The Jailer's Surprise

Storyline **Louise Moon**
Illustrations **Steven Butler**

After his conversion, Paul traveled from town to town with his new friend Silas.

He loved to tell others about Jesus, and many
became believers. But not everyone was pleased.

In one city, a slave girl kept following them and
shouting. Paul told the evil spirit to come out of her.

The girl's owners were very angry because now she could no longer make money by telling fortunes.

Paul and Silas were hauled before the magistrates.
The crowd claimed they were troublemakers.

The magistrates ordered that Paul and Silas were
to be beaten, and then put into prison.

The angry magistrates told the jailer to watch Paul and Silas carefully so they could not escape.

So the jailer locked Paul and Silas in an inner cell.
Just to be safe he put chains on them, too.

Even though they were in a terrible place, Paul and Silas began to pray and sing praises to God.

The other prisoners listened in surprise. Far into the night, the singing and praying continued.

Suddenly, there was a rumble, RUMBLE, RUMBLE!
The prison shook in a violent earthquake!

Bang, bang! Crash, crash! The cell doors flew
open and everyone's chains came off.

The jailer woke and thought all the prisoners had escaped. He took his sword to kill himself.

"Wait!" cried Paul. "Don't hurt yourself! We are all here." They all came slowly forward.

The jailer called for lights, then he rushed
in and fell before Paul and Silas.

He brought them out of the prison and fell at their feet. "What must I do to be saved?" he asked.

Even though it was the middle of the night,
Paul and Silas told the jailer all about Jesus.

And before the night was over, the jailer and everyone in his family prayed to Jesus.

Then the jailer brought Paul and Silas into his house and gently washed their wounds.

He gave them some food, and the family was happy because God loved them.

The next day, the magistrates were afraid.
They knew what they had done was wrong.

They came to the prison to see Paul and Silas,
and very politely asked them to leave.

So Paul and Silas left that town, but they
continued to tell everyone about Jesus.